Sue Wilson is going to
a business meeting.

Mr Stacey is taking his children
on a day out during their
half-term holiday.
"Come on," he says.
"Let's go and buy the tickets."

3

"How much will that be?" he asks at the Ticket Office.

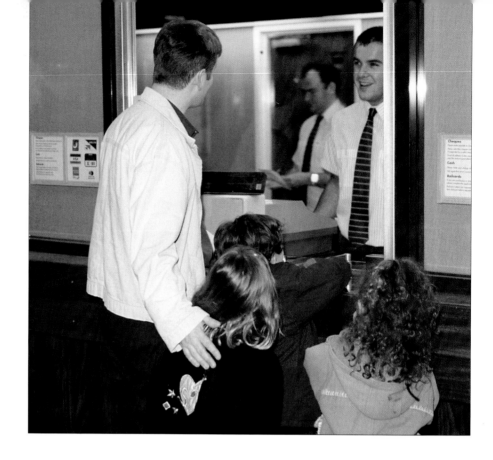

Mr Stacey puts the money on the turn-table, and the cashier gives him the tickets to travel.

Mr Stacey and the children look at the departure board. "Which is our train, Dad?" asks Sian. "There it is," says their father. "It's going from Platform 3."

Departures

nation	Plat.	Expld time	Calling at
CHR AIR	3	1023	LEEDS DEWSBURY HUDDERSFLD MANCHR PIC MANCHESTER AIRPORT
BY	1	1022	SELBY
CHR VIC	6	1024	MICKLFLD E.GARFORTH GARFORTH CROSSGATES LEEDS BRAMLEY NEW PUDSEY BRADFORD HALIFAX AND PRINCIPAL STATIONS VIA ROCHDALE TO MANCHR VIC
DON KX	3	1032	DONCASTER PETERBORO LONDON KX
ERPOOL	10	1037	LEEDS HUDDERSFLD STALYBRDG MANCHR PIC OXFORD RD. BIRCHWOOD WARRINGTON LIVERPOOL
RBORO	5	1038	MALTON SEAMER SCARBORO
ZANCE	9	1042	LEEDS WAKEFIELD SHEFFIELD DERBY BIRMINGHAM BRISTOL TM TAUNTON EXETER STD PLYMOUTH LISKEARD BODMIN PKW PAR ST.AUSTELL TRURO REDRUTH CAMBORNE ST. ERTH PENZANCE
DERLAND	5	1045	NORTHALLTN DARLINGTON DURHAM NEWCASTLE SUNDERLAND

The Stacey family have plenty of time
before their train leaves.
They go to the coffee shop
to have a snack.
"Ooh, look - doughnuts!" says Natasha.

Miss Wilson checks the time of her train. One of the station's Welcome Team points to the indicator board to show her the train she needs to catch.

Sue goes to the waiting room to read her newspaper.

Meanwhile, in the Telephone Enquiry Office, the clerks are busy taking customers' calls.

They give people information
about the many different trains that travel
across the country.

The staff in the Travel Centre
give information to customers
already at the station.
"Can I have the times of trains
to Liverpool?" one lady asks.
The assistant looks at his computer screen
and tells her the details she needs.

On Platform 2 a train
has reached the end
of its journey.
The cleaners go into action.
They collect the newspapers
and rubbish that the passengers
have left behind.

On Platform 10 the Royal Mail staff
are loading the post on to the train.
They use a ramp to help them move
the heavy sacks of mail.
"There's a lot here today, Mac,"
says Tom.

Rail express systems

On another platform
a Welcome Host is helping a customer.
"We need a porter and wheelchair
on Platform 5," says the Welcome Host
on her mobile phone.

A porter comes to carry the lady's luggage and one of the Platform Staff pushes her disabled friend on to the train.

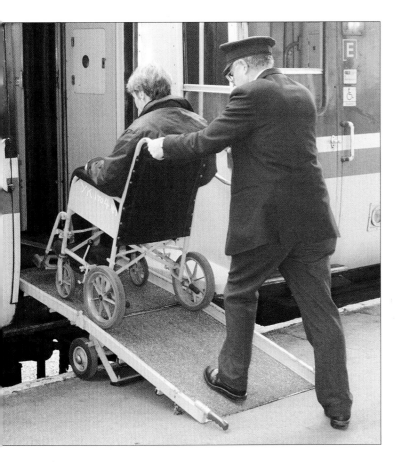

People are busy in other parts of the station, too. The police make their regular patrol of the platforms, and travellers draw money from the cashpoint machines.

Outside the station,
passengers who have just arrived
queue up for taxis.
"Can you take me to
The Star Hotel, please?"
one man asks the driver.

In the Control Room
the Signal Man
studies the computer screens.
These show him which trains
are on the move and
exactly where they are.

The Announcer speaks into
the microphone to tell
the passengers in the station
when trains are arriving.
"The train approaching Platform 3
is the 10.32 to London," she says.

Miss Wilson hears the announcement. She leaves the waiting room to catch her train.

Danny is one of the Train Dispatch Staff. He talks to the Supervisor on his radio. The Supervisor tells Danny of any problems or information about the approaching train.

The train arrives at Platform 3.
The passengers pick up their bags
and prepare to board the train.

"Is this the 10.32 to London?"
asks a man who has just arrived.
"Yes, sir," says Danny.
"It leaves in five minutes' time."

Miss Wilson boards the train. She looks for a seat near a table so that she can do her work on the journey.

Mr Stacey and the children quickly jump on to the train.
Once all the doors are shut Danny blows his whistle.
"It's time to go," says Mr Stacey.
The train slowly moves away.

Care and safety in a station

When you are in a busy station it is important to make sure that you and others keep safe.

Try to remember some of these tips:

1. Always keep well away from the edge of the platform.

2. Never go near a railway track. Only cross by a bridge.

3. If you drop something on the line, don't jump down and get it.

4. Never get off a moving train.

5. Always stay close to your parent or friend.

Index

© 1997 Franklin Watts
This edition 2002

Franklin Watts, 96 Leonard Street
London EC2A 4XD

Franklin Watts Australia
56 O'Riordan Street
Alexandria, Sydney, NSW 2015

ISBN 0 7496 4557 1 (pbk)

Dewey Decimal Classification 385

A CIP catalogue record for this book is
available from the British Library

Printed in Hong Kong

Editor: Samantha Armstrong
Designer: Kirstie Billingham
Photographer: Harry Cory-Wright
Illustrations: Kim Woolley

With thanks to Nigel, Natasha and Sian
Stacey, Henry Fothergill, Sue Wilson and
all at GNER, York.